The Loyal Customer:

A Lesson From a Cab Driver

by
Shep Hyken

The Alan Press

The Loyal Customer:
A Lesson From a Cab Driver
by
Shep Hyken

For information contact:
The Alan Press
C/O Shep Hyken
11622 Ladue Road
St. Louis, MO 63141
(314) 692-2200
Fax: (314) 692-2222
Email: shep@hyken.com
www.hyken.com

Library of Congress Catalog Number: 98-095028

ISBN: 0-9637820-1-0

Printed in the United States of America

9 8 7 6 5 4 3 2

Also by Shep Hyken

Moments of Magic

Only the Best On Success

Only the Best On Leadership

Only the Best On Customer Service

The Winning Spirit

Inspiring Others to Win

Service: Creating Moments of Magic (Video Learning System)

To order contact Shep Hyken at:

(314) 692-2200
(800) 829-3888
Email: shep@hyken.com
www.hyken.com

Acknowledgments

The first person I must acknowledge is Frank, my Dallas cab driver. Over the years he has been an inspiration to what customer service and loyalty is all about. This man had it figured out. We will all learn from him.

Another person I want to thank is my brother, Rusty Hyken. Rusty is an English teacher and did the final proof. He told me that I could blame him for any grammar or spelling mistakes that are in the book. Thanks Rusty! I feel liberated!

A special thanks to Bob Bangart, who designed a fun cover for the book. Bob is a fun guy to be around. He has great energy and even greater creativity.

Thanks to my audiences. There have been hundreds of audiences with thousands and thousands of people. The applause and laughter throughout the story of Frank have validated that it is an entertaining story, but the comments and letters after the speeches validate the important lesson we learn from the story.

There are my speaking and writing buddies. These are my business peers. There are just too many to name, but you know who you are. We have helped guide each other to higher levels in our profession.

Finally, I must acknowledge my family. My wife, Cindy, and my three children, Brian, Alex and Casey make life worth living. They support the efforts I make in my career and put up with my crazy travel schedule. They have taught me how to "stop and smell the roses." And, they are my roses!

Table of Contents

Preface

Don't think of this as a book. This may look like a book, feel like a book, and even cost like a book. But, try not to think of this as a book.

Think of this as a lesson. Whatever you may have paid for these pages or whatever time you spend reading them, that is an investment for a lesson.

This story is very focused. There is only one point -- creating the loyal customer.

I plan to share with you a true story that illustrates the concept, and then back it up with practical logic and reason to show you how and why it works.

While I use Frank, a cab driver from Dallas, Texas as the example, this information is applicable to any and every type of business.

I know you will find this lesson a valuable use of your time and hope you are able to put the ideas to use for yourself.

Remember, this is not a book. It's a lesson!

Introduction

In the words of Jack Webb from the television show *Dragnet*...

"The story you are about to read is true. The names have been changed to protect the innocent."

I am a professional speaker. I travel around the world presenting speeches, primarily, in the area of customer service, relations and loyalty. The story you are about to read is a true story. It actually happened to me a number of years ago. Since then, I have told the story hundreds of times in my speeches and programs.

Many times people come up to me after the speech and ask me if the story about Frank, the cab driver, is real. Absolutely!

Let me repeat. The story is true, but you should also know this:

The interview with Frank in Part II of this lesson is not real. It is fiction - creative writing!

As a speaker and author, I have taken creative license to invent the interview in Part II to help you understand Frank's success and better illustrate the concept and lesson you are about to learn.

So, spend the next few minutes reading the story and the interview. Then take the time to complete the "self study" questions, and be prepared to learn a lesson that may help change the way you do business forever!

THE STORY

It was a great day. I had just finished speaking to a group of executives who were meeting for their semi-annual company meeting. The applause was sweet, and when I stepped off of the stage, the conference planner gave me a "thumbs up" and mouthed the words "home run."

After spending about a half an hour answering questions from a few of the audience members, it was time to get a cab and head to the airport.

The conference was being held at the Dallas Convention Center, about 25 minutes from the airport, provided there aren't any traffic problems. My flight wasn't leaving for almost two hours, so I was very relaxed. I picked up my luggage and briefcase and headed for the door.

This particular day was extraordinarily hot. The temperature was 102 degrees, and the humidity seemed to be almost 100 percent even though it wasn't raining. I was wearing a business suit and when I stepped outside, it seemed as if someone had thrown a bucket of water on me.

Within a minute a cab pulled up to the curb where I stood. Out jumped the driver. He came around the back of the cab to take my bags and put them in the trunk. I took one look at this guy and thought to myself, "This is a moment of misery! Look at this guy. He has cut off-shorts, a torn sleeveless shirt, messed up hair. And, he probably hasn't shaved in at least a week. Maybe, he hasn't even showered in a week! He looks like a bum!"

I thought, "It is 102 degrees out here, what is it like in his cab? There probably isn't any air conditioning, and the cab has to be filthy dirty. I'll get out to the airport 25 minutes from now, my suit will be drenched in sweat and it will be wrinkled and trashed for the day. And, about the time I get out of the cab, a little spring is going to pop through the vinyl seat and rip my pants." Talk about bad luck! I couldn't believe that I was going to have to ride in this guy's cab.

He looked at me wondering why I was looking at him so closely. Then he said in a deep Texas accent that sounded nothing like the man I was looking at, "Get in the cab. It is nice and cool inside the cab. I'll take care of the bags."

It didn't sound like him. I even thought it was weird. I looked behind the cab to see if there was a ventriloquist throwing his voice, but there was no one there. So, I did what he said and handed him the bags to put in the trunk.

When I opened the door, cool air hit me in the face. It was almost cold in the cab. The air conditioner was blowing as hard as it probably could. When I sat down, I noticed that the cab was not just clean, but meticulous. Neatly folded on the seat were two newspapers, the local Dallas paper and a USA Today. On the "hump" in the middle of the car was a bucket of ice with two soft drinks. I couldn't believe this could really be this guy's cab. I

17

even looked back to make sure he was actually putting the bags in the back of the cab! (He was.)

Eventually he got in the cab, picked up a plate of candy and turned around to offer me a piece. That is when I remembered what Mom used to say, "Don't ever take candy from strangers!"

But, I took the candy anyway and asked the driver, "Is this your cab or are you borrowing it for the day?"

He replied, "This is my cab. Make yourself at home. The candy is yours to eat. The sodas are yours to drink. The newspapers are yours to read and take with you at the end of the trip if you would like. And, if you need to call the office, I have a car phone. By the way, there is no extra charge for any of this. It is all compliments of me. And, I charge the same $22.00 flat rate that any other cab driver would charge to take you from downtown to the airport. Sit back and enjoy the ride."

I was amazed!

When we finally got out to the highway he asked me a question that no other cab driver had ever asked me before. "Are you in a hurry, or is it okay if I do the speed limit?"

What kind of a cab driver is this! Usually they fly down the highway, getting from point A to point B as fast as they can so they can pick up another fare and make more money. But not this guy. By that time I was reading his paper and drinking a soda. I said, "Take your time."

He was pointing out a few of the sights along the way, creating small talk and making pleasant conversation. Then he asked me, "Have you ever seen the famous fountain at Las Colinas?"

I replied, "I think I've seen a picture of it."

He got excited. "If you haven't seen it, I have to show it to you. It is just up the road a ways. Right on the way to the airport and not even a mile off the highway. It is probably the most beautiful place in all of Dallas. It might even be the most beautiful fountain in the entire United States. I would love to show it to you, and I won't charge you any extra

19

money. It will be the same $22.00 flat rate. Would you like to see the fountain?"

He was obviously very excited, so I thought I would humor him and said enthusiastically, "Show me the fountain!"

He became overly enthusiastic and stepped on the gas to speed us up. He pulled off of the highway, and, in less than a minute, the cab screeched to a halt in front of the famous fountain at Las Colinas.

He jumped out of the cab and opened my door for me. He helped me out -- so excited he almost yanked me out of the cab. A moment later we were standing before one of the most beautiful fountains I had ever seen. There were larger than life size statues of horses running across water, and, where their hooves hit the water, there were splashes. These statues looked so lifelike that you could actually sense energy and motion coming from them. This was the famous "Mustangs at Las Colinas" sculpted by Robert Glen.

We eventually got back into the car, and the driver said, "By the way, my name is Frank. Do you have a business card? I collect the business cards of the people that I drive."

I said, "Sure Frank. My name is Shep." I handed him my card, and he handed me his.

Frank said, "You may notice that there are a few phone numbers on the card. You have the cab company's phone number. And, if you want me, you have my personal home phone number and my car phone number. You can always reach me at one of those. The next time you come back to Dallas give me a call a day or two ahead of time. Let me know what time you are coming in, what airline and flight number you are on and I'll pick you up. I'll treat you like a limousine driver but charge you the same flat rate of the cab. I'll even park the car outside, come inside and meet you at the gate. When you walk off that airplane, I'll be standing there ready to take your bags. Don't worry, you'll recognize me."

I said, "You can count on that." I was thinking to myself, "Wow! This guy is good!"

Eventually we made it to the airport, and I gave him a nice tip. Most drivers would get a few dollars, but I gave him thirty bucks and told him to keep the change. He showed an appreciative smile, said, "Good bye. I hope to see you again when you are back in Dallas."

I said, "Plan on it."

The reason this is a good story is because with the exception of the first impression, everything else was a wonderful experience. Much better than average and obviously memorable. But, there is a serious lesson to be learned. Most cab drivers "manage" the experience of their customers pretty well. If they have a clean cab and drive safely, the customer will usually leave a nice tip of ten to fifteen percent. And, that is the end of it.

Most likely, the customer will probably never see the cab driver again.

Frank, however, had a different goal. He wanted to see his customers again, and he went out of his way to make sure it happened. He didn't just manage the passenger's experience, he created it. Frank added to the typical passenger experience. He had the newspapers, the sodas, the candy, the car phone and the trip to Las Colinas. I couldn't wait to get back to Dallas to see what Frank had in store for me next.

So, this is a good story, but it is not the whole story. Now as the great radio personality, Paul Harvey, says... "Here is the rest of the story!"

Four days after this trip to Dallas, I was in my office and opened that day's mail. There was a thank you note from Frank, my cab driver.

A thank you note from a cab driver! Unbelievable! I had never received a thank you note from a cab driver before. This was unheard of!

Every Christmas I would also get a Christmas card from Frank and his wife!

Well, you can probably guess the end of the story -- at least part of it. You know I went back to Dallas and always used my "regular" cab driver -- until he retired from the business and moved on to something else.

Frank became very successful. He was making almost five times more money than most of the other Dallas cab drivers. He had figured out a formula for success.

Allow me to invite you to the interview where Frank reveals all of his secrets for success.

Mr. Hyken,

    Just a note to let you know how much I appreciated your business while you were in Dallas.

    Please contact me a few days in advance of your next visit so that I can arrange to meet you at the airport.

    Thanks again,

    Frank

THE INTERVIEW

SHEP: Frank, about ten years ago you started driving a cab for a living, and today you no longer do that. What are you doing now?

FRANK: Well, you need to know what I used to do before I was a cab driver. I used to work for a small telephone company that sold phone systems to small businesses. I was the chief repair and installation guy. This was a very small company. The owner not only ran the business, but also was the sales person. He'd sell 'em and I'd install 'em.

This guy liked to cut corners. For example, he sold a pretty decent phone but used the cheapest materials to install it. The wiring and phone jacks were the worst you could buy. And you can probably guess what would happen. The wires would short out, and the phones wouldn't work.

SHEP: So, what did you do?

FRANK: I didn't do anything until my boss told me to do it. The customers would call him to complain. He was slow to get back to them. And when he did get back to them, he would argue. Most of the customers were pretty persistent and insisted that he send someone out to get the phones working.

SHEP: And, that someone was you?

FRANK: That's right. By the time I showed up at their offices, they were worked-up and angry. It wasn't much fun. All my boss had to do when they first called was say he was sorry and get me out to their office as fast as possible. Instead he chose to argue with them, but he still had to send me out. I can't understand why he did that.

SHEP: But, what about the reason for the problem in the first place? Don't you think most of this could have been avoided if he hadn't used those shoddy materials?

FRANK: That is something I could never understand. I may not be the sharpest business man, but I know this. The cost of decent wire and jacks is a fraction of what it cost him to send me out to fix the phone system. Worst part was that when he sent me to fix it, he sent me with the same cheap wire that caused the problem in the first place. I can't understand what he was thinking.

SHEP: I think I know. He was probably thinking of just that sale and how much money he could make on that one transaction. He didn't give any thought to the future value of his customer. He missed out on the fact that his small business customers might one day get bigger and expand or even upgrade their equipment.

FRANK: No kidding!

SHEP: So, how did you decide to become a cab driver?

FRANK: That's easy. I didn't like the way my boss treated the customers, and I didn't like the way he treated me. And when he didn't treat his customers right, they took it out on me. Hey, I was just doing my job. So, I just quit on him. Told him I didn't like the way he did business, and that was that. I looked around for another job in the same line of work. Until I found one, I decided to drive a cab.

I grew up in Dallas, been here all of my life, and knew my way around pretty well, so I went to work for this cab company. It was like having my own business. I would rent the cab for the day. The rent would cover the company's costs for maintaining the cab and insuring the cab. I had to pay for my own gas. I got to keep the cab for twelve hours. During that time a driver could work as hard or as little as he wanted. It was up to me. It was like I was in business for myself.

SHEP: So you saw it as sort of a franchise? Your own business?

FRANK: Sure! And if a driver was really good at maintaining the cab, the company would sometimes let him keep the cab over-night. Otherwise the company had to clean and maintain the cab themselves. I could never be sure that I would get the same cab. So I made sure that the cab was always super clean. That is what worked best for me.

SHEP: That was also good for business. Your customers had to appreciate how clean your cab was.

FRANK: Oh yes. I was in control.

SHEP: You once told me you made four to five times more money than the average cab driver in Dallas. How did you do that?

FRANK: Some might say I'm lucky. I do admit that I have pretty good luck.

At first I did what every other cab driver does. I would go to the airport and wait in the line with all of the other drivers. Some days it was miserable. We would get there and sometimes have to wait over three hours in the boiling hot sun, just to get a fare that might be only a few miles away. It was like we were making just two or three dollars an hour. Then most of us would drop the passengers off and high tail it back to the airport, just to wait another two or three hours to get another lousy fare. On those bad days we might not even get enough fares to cover the cost of renting our cab.

SHEP: So, how did you make the money?

FRANK: I'm get'n to it. Like I said, I got lucky.

I knew that I wanted to keep the cab super clean so I could drive home in it every night and keep the same cab, but I didn't realize how it would affect the customer. I found that my customers would comment to me about how new and clean my cab was. They were shocked when I told them there was over 80,000 miles on it. I told them how the first time I got the cab it was a pit. A real mess. It took me two weeks to get it to where it looked like it did. And, it was a lot of work to keep it looking that good. But, it got me an extra buck or two when it came time to get my tip.

SHEP: What about the newspapers and sodas?

FRANK: That was lucky too. One day I had a newspaper. One of my customers asked if he could read it. I was done with it so I said sure, go ahead. I even told him he could keep it. The guy thanked me, and I got the biggest tip I ever got at the end of a trip.

I thought to myself, "I ought to have a newspaper for every one of my customers."

It wasn't long after that, that one of my fares asked for my number. He liked how clean the cab was and appreciated the newspaper and wanted me to pick him up after his business meeting and take him back to the airport.

SHEP: And, the rest is history!

FRANK: Not so fast. I didn't have a car phone, so there was no way for this guy to call me direct. Even though he called the cab company and asked for me, my company dispatched a different driver.

But, I figured it out quickly. I missed an opportunity to get a decent fare and not have to wait in the airport line. So, I got a car phone and had some business cards printed up with my car and home phone numbers. I offered the card to every one of my passengers. And, you know what? Some of them started to call me back.

SHEP: What about the sodas?

FRANK: Well, it really started with coffee. One day one of my customers called me for an early morning pickup. I stopped at the gas station to fill up and bought some coffee for myself. Then I thought, why not do something nice and buy one for my customer?

This guy was so nice. I gave him a newspaper and a cup of coffee. He gave me a five dollar tip on a ten dollar fare!

That newspaper and coffee only cost me about a buck. The way I look at it, I might have only gotten a buck tip. Instead I got five - even though it cost me a buck. You do the math.

SHEP: You confirmed an old customer service adage. "Great service doesn't cost, it pays!"

FRANK: I learned a lot in a short period of time. All of a sudden I wasn't waiting in line at the airport very often. Most of my trips were calling me. No more lines!

Coffee was hard to keep warm, and not

everyone wanted coffee throughout the day. But, most appreciated a cold soda. And, I could keep a cooler up front with me to keep stocking my little drink caddy.

SHEP: Drink caddy?

FRANK: That is the little bucket with the sand bags on the sides to keep it from moving around. I just keep the little bucket iced with a couple of sodas, and the customers think they are being treated to a limousine ride.

And, get this. My reputation started to catch on at the hotels. These sharp doorman would tell their hotel guests about me, and they were making an extra buck or two when I showed up to take care of them. And, they would give me their left over newspapers. Most of the time I wouldn't have to buy the newspapers!

SHEP: What about the fountain at Las Colinas? I remember giving a few of my friends your name and number and you took them to the airport. They all told me you showed them the fountain. Did you show everybody the fountain?

FRANK: That's just part of my Texas hospitality. I love that place. I wanted everyone to enjoy it. I was proud to show everyone that fountain. If they wanted, I'd show them other places too.

SHEP: And, all of us got a thank you note every time you drove us.

FRANK: That was my wife's idea. She's a pretty smart woman. You know, it doesn't take much time to write a short note. I usually would do it while I was waiting for my next customer. Once in a while I'd start to get behind, and she would help me, but I learned to be pretty good at keeping up with them. As good and comfortable I could make the cab for my passengers, it was probably the thank you notes that kept bringing people back. It was like the icing on the cake.

SHEP: You made quite a bit of money doing this, didn't you?

FRANK: Yes I did. I was paid well for the extra effort I took to make my customers want to keep coming back. I made great tips, had repeat business and hardly ever had to

36

wait for a passenger. I had lots of appoint-
ments. From what I could tell, I made four to
five times what the average cab driver was
making here in Dallas.

SHEP: Did you ever have so much business
you couldn't handle it all?

FRANK: Within a short time that became a
big problem. But I had a bunch of friends who
also drove cabs, and they really appreciated
me sending them some of my fares.

SHEP: Were they able to give your customers the same level of service?

FRANK: That was my biggest headache.
There was no way for me to guarantee that.
At first I thought I could make money from
giving them business. They would give me a
few bucks for every trip I gave them.
But, some of them weren't treating the customers the way I liked to treat them. They
didn't always have a newspaper or whatever.
So, the deal I made with them was that they
had to have the same kind of service I
provided, or I wouldn't refer anybody to
them. And, I stopped asking them for a cut
of the fare. In the beginning, I asked them

for a small cut.

SHEP: Did it work?

FRANK: It weeded out the ones who didn't want to go the extra mile real fast.

SHEP: How did you know if they were doing a good job?

FRANK: My wife checked on them. We would call the customers back a few days later and make sure they were taken care of by my buddies. If not, then we never referred any business to them again.

SHEP: So, your wife was in on all of it.

FRANK: My wife taught me a lot about how I do business. She used to hear me complain when I would come home after working at the phone company. She encouraged me to quit the phone company and start doing something that gave me more control over the situation.

SHEP: But, where did you learn to treat the customers so well?

FRANK: That was some of my wife's doing too. She said that I should treat my customers with respect and dignity. Basically the way I would want to be treated, and for sure the way they would want to be treated.

SHEP: You've made a lot of money as a cab driver. Much more than the average driver. All of this was due to big tips from loyal customers.

FRANK: I have to emphasize that it was more than just loyal customers. It was having **lots** of loyal customers. I made bigger tips and hardly ever waited in lines. If I wasn't driving the customer, I was going to pick someone up. Like I said before, I wasn't waiting for hours at the airport line. I was only waiting five or ten minutes for my customer to come out of a meeting. There was hardly any downtime.

SHEP: And, now you don't drive a cab anymore do you?

FRANK: Nope!

SHEP: I would think that by now you would own the cab company or a limousine service.

FRANK: I guess I had what you could call a limousine service. I just used a cab to do it. I was better than the typical cab driver. I gave more for the money and treated the customers the way they wanted to be treated. I was reliable and always on time.

SHEP: So what do you do now?

FRANK: It was the proudest day in my life. I had saved-up some pretty good money. We don't have kids, and my wife and I have a pretty simple life. I thought about the phone company. I really did like doing that type of work. It was fun and interesting. You got to meet all kinds of nice people in all types of different businesses. I just didn't like the way my boss treated me or the customers. So, I went back and talked to my old boss. It had been a few years. He was just barely getting by. I made him an offer. I told him I wanted to buy the company.

SHEP: You bought your former boss out of his business?

FRANK: It didn't take much. He had some equipment and good contacts for supplies.

The only thing wrong with his company was him. Take him out of the company and replace him with my wife, and we have the friendliest little phone company around!

SHEP: How does it compare to the cab business?

FRANK: Much better. First, the hours are a little better. I don't find myself picking people up on Christmas and other holidays. And, we have some great customers. They keep getting us more business with people they know. Just like when I drove a cab, most of the business we get comes from word of mouth. We've had to add people. We have someone who takes care of the books, two more sales people and three more technicians to work with me. It has become bigger than we thought, but it is still a lot of fun.

SHEP: Well Frank, you sure have done a great job. Most people wouldn't take the time or effort to go the extra mile that you did for your customers. It is commendable.

FRANK: Everybody thinks I went to a lot of trouble to do this. Hey, it didn't take any time at all. Maybe a few minutes. Mostly, I was just being nice and treating people the way they wanted to be treated.

SHEP: Even though it was a small effort, it was still something extra. I've always said that the biggest difference between successful people and those that aren't is that successful people are willing to do what unsuccessful people aren't willing to do. I don't care how small the effort is or how little time it takes, it is still something extra.

Frank, I want to thank you for your time and the lessons you shared with us today. Your story is one that should be admired by all people in business. Thanks for your words of wisdom.

FRANK: You flatter me. Thank you!

WHAT WE HAVE LEARNED

THE ULTIMATE LESSON: There is a difference between satisfied customers and loyal customers.

I hope you have learned from Frank. Most of us can relate to this story because most of us have been in a taxi cab. The image most people conjure up of a typical cab is not a great one. Usually it is a New York cab on a hot muggy day, stuck in traffic, horn blowing, with the driver cursing at the car next to him.

However, this is not usually the case. Most people have a relatively good experience when they take a cab. Usually the cab is fairly clean and the driver is courteous and gets you to where you want safely. Then, you give the cab driver a tip...

And NEVER see the cab driver again!

If you had to rate your experience in the cab you would probably rate it as satisfactory.

If there is only one thing you remember from this lesson, remember this...

There is a big difference between a satisfied customer and a loyal customer!

Most cab drivers manage their customers' experience for satisfactory results. A moderately clean cab, safe ride and maybe some pleasant conversation -- that is it.

With the exception of the first impression (So, Frank doesn't know how to dress for success!), Frank did more than manage the experience. He created or manufactured it. He added the candy, sodas, newspapers, etc. By doing so, he exceeded his customers' expectations.

It doesn't matter if you are a banker, broker, consultant, sales person, grocery store checker, baseball announcer, secretary, airline pilot, bartender - I can go on and on! What can you do to go beyond simple management of your customer's experience? What can you do to create/manufacture an experience that exceeds their expectations? Sometimes all it takes is the right attitude. Other times it takes just a little extra effort. Not a lot! But, just a little, which is usually more than the competition is doing.

If whatever you sell does what it is supposed to do - maybe even better than it is suppose to - the way to make it even better is to couple it with a higher level of service.

The type of service that Frank provided his customers wasn't stuff you learn from a text book in a college class. It was just common sense. Remember what he said? "Mostly I was just treating my customers with respect and dignity. Basically, the way I would want to be treated and for sure the way they would want to be treated."

So simple!

Self Study

If you are on this page, most likely
you have read the book. However,
just reading it isn't going to do you any good.
You have to do something with the information.

Maybe you have learned something
about customer loyalty by now, but
that isn't enough. It is said that
knowledge is power. But, really it
is how you use the knowledge that
gives you real power.

The following questions are designed to help you use the knowledge
you have learned from this lesson.
Don't just think about the answers.
Write them down -- with lots of detail!

1. What are you currently doing, if anything, to create the **"Wow!"** effect, similar to what Frank did for his customers? Does your competition do the same thing?

2. Do you know of anything that your competition is doing differently than you that creates extra value for their customers? (By the way, don't copy them. Use what they are doing as a starting point for you to improve on.)

3. Think about the "chain of events" that happens when you are in a cab. First, the cab pulls up or is waiting. The driver may get out to greet you and help with your luggage. You get in the cab. You are driven to your destination. There may be some verbal inter-action along the way. You arrive at your destination. You pay the driver. He/she may help you out of the cab, get your luggage , etc. What is the typical "chain of events" that takes place with the people you do business with? (Be very specific and detailed.)

4. Is there a weak link in your "chain" that could cause a problem or complaint? (This problem could come from people, policy or procedure, accounting, lack of training, etc.)

5. Following up on question number 4, if there is a weak link in your "chain," what can you do to eliminate it?

6. Is there a particular place in your "chain" that you can strengthen to create more loyalty? (Frank had newspapers, candy, the cell phone, etc.)

7. After reading this lesson and answering these questions, what are you going to do that you haven't been doing before?

Recommended Reading

Customers for Life by Carl Sewell and Paul Brown; Doubleday 1990

Customer Satisfaction Is Worthless, Customer Loyalty Is Priceless by Jeffrey H. Gitomer; Bard Press 1998

How to Win Customers and Keep Them For Life by Michael LeBoeuf; Berkley 1987

Inside the Magic Kingdom by Tom Connellan; Bard Press 1996

The Loyalty Effect by Frederick F. Reichheld; Harvard Business School Press 1996

Moments of Magic by Shep Hyken; The Alan Press 1996

Moments of Truth by Jan Carlzon; Harper & Row 1987

Positively Outrageous Service by T. Scott Gross; Warner Books 1994

The Quest for Service Quality by Phil Wexler; Maxcomm Associates 1993

Raving Fans by Kenneth Blanchard (and anything else Ken has written); William Morrow & Company 1993

The Real Heroes of Business by Bill Fromm and Len Schlesinger; Doubleday 1993

Selling the Invisible by Harry Beckwith; Warner Books 1997

Swim With the Sharks Without Being Eaten Alive by Harvey Mackay (and anything else Harvey has written); William Morrow & Company 1988

Other Books and Products by Shep Hyken

Moments of Magic
158 page book................................$12.95
Shep's best seller! A clearly written, easy-to-read, easy to understand guide to customer service for anyone in any job. It is filled with information, techniques, and stories that will teach you to deliver excellent service to your internal and outside customers.

The Winning Spirit
198 page book................................$16.95
Published in cooperation with the United States Olympic Committee, twenty experts wrote on "achieving Olympic level performance in business and personal advancements." Authors include Shep Hyken (Gold Medal Customer Service), Frank Mcguire, Don Hutson, Tony Alessandra, Jim Tunney, Les Brown and more!

Inspiring Others to Win
186 page book................................$16.95
Second in the series of "Olympic" books, this was also, published in cooperation with the

United States Olympic Committee. Twenty of the best speakers in the industry write on mentoring, coaching and inspiring people to greater levels of performance. Authors include Shep Hyken (Nobody Does It On Their Own), Tony Alessandra, Warren Greshes, Jim Cathcart, Don Hutson and more!

Only the BEST On Success
198 page book..$11.95
If you like *Only the BEST On Customer Service,* you will love this book. Motivation and success are what this book is about featuring Shep Hyken writing on *You Are The Magic!* as well as other inspiring authors such as Roger Crawford, Mark Sanborn, Keith Harrell and more!

Only the Best on Leadership
172 page book..$11.95
The second in the *Only the Best* series focuses on leadership and features Shep Hyken's chapter on *The Top Ten Traits of Great Leadership.* Other authors include Larry Winget, Scott McKain and more!

Only the Best on Customer Service
224 page book..$11.95
The third in the *Only the Best* series focuses

on customer service and opens with Shep Hyken's chapter on *Seven Ways To Customer Loyalty.* Other authors include Larry Winget, Scott McKain, Keith Harrell and more!

Service: Creating Moments of Magic
2 videos & workbook....................................$99.00
A video learning system with a focus on internal and external customers. The workbook includes exercises that will personalize the information to the viewer's day-to-day responsibilities. Additional workbooks are only $5.00 each. An outstanding tool!

The Loyal Customer: A Lesson From A Cab Driver by Shep Hyken
50 page lesson (looks like a book)..................8.95
Hey, you are holding it in your hands! Want to buy one for a friend? Or, how about a bunch for your business? Remember, it is not a book. It is a lesson!

For information on ordering,
just turn the page!

Ordering is easy!

Just write on a piece of paper what you want to order and fax or mail to the address below.

Please add $5.00 shipping & handling for U.S. orders. (Please contact us for orders outside of the United States.)

We accept Mastercard, Visa and American Express. Be sure to include the expiration date.

Call regarding quantity discounts.

To get more information on Shep Hyken's keynote presentations and seminars, please contact:

Shep Hyken
Shepard Presentations
711 Old Ballas Rd., Suite 215
St. Louis, MO 63141
(800) 829-3888 or (314) 692-2200
FAX: (314) 692-2222
E Mail: shep@hyken.com
http://www.hyken.com/

About the Author

Shep Hyken, CSP is a speaker and author who has been entertaining audiences with his unique presentation style for over 25 years. He worked as a comic/magician in high school and college. In 1983 made the transition from entertainer to speaker. Shep mixes information with entertainment (humor and magic) to create exciting programs.

Shep's most requested programs focus on customer loyalty and service, internal service, customer relations, and a motivational program titled "You Are The Magic!"

Shep has worked with hundreds of companies and associations ranging from "Fortune 500" size companies to smaller organizations with less than 50 employees. Some of his clients include American Express, Abbott Laboratories, Avis, AIG, American Airlines, Aetna Insurance, Anheuser-Busch, AT&T, Arthur Andersen, — and that is just a few of the A's!

(CSP stands for Certified Speaking Professional, a designation awarded by the National Speakers Association to individuals for certain achievements and education in the speaking profession.)